Snowboarding

Chuck Miller

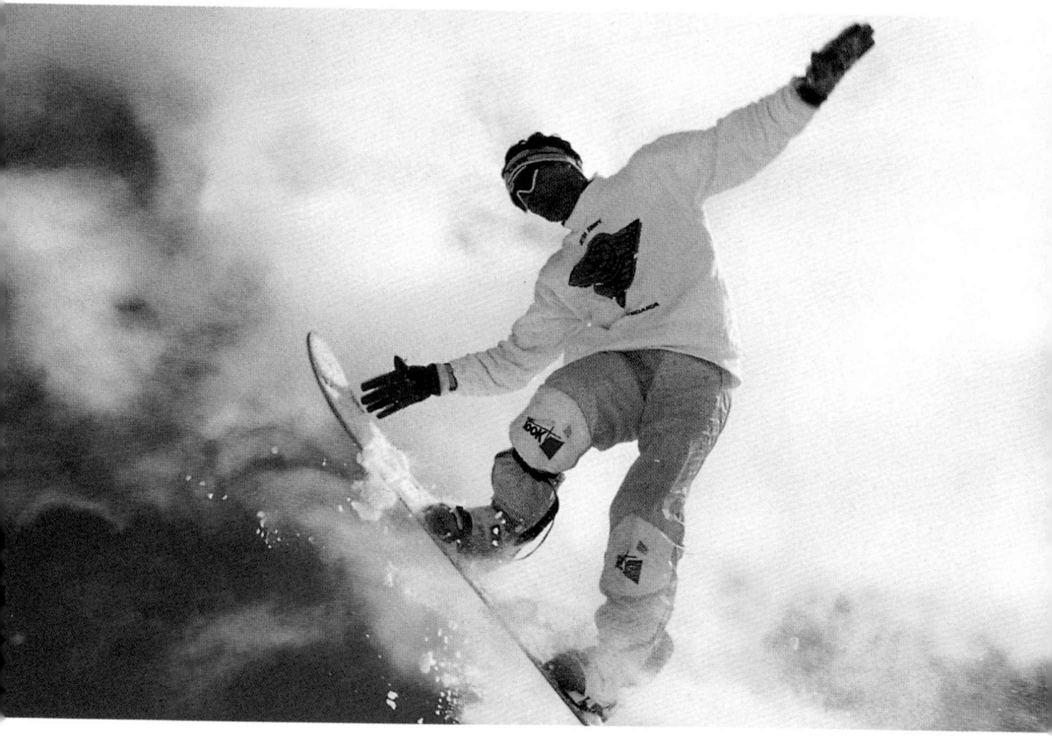

www.raintreepublishers.co.uk

Visit our website to find out more information about **Raintree** books.

To order:
☎ Phone 44 (0) 1865 888112
🖷 Send a fax to 44 (0) 1865 314091
🖳 Visit the Raintree Bookshop at www.raintreepublishers.co.uk to browse our catalogue and order online.

First published in Great Britain by Raintree Publishers, Halley Court, Jordan Hill, Oxford, OX2 8EJ, part of Harcourt Education.
Raintree is a registered trademark of Harcourt Education Ltd.

Consultant: Gregg Davis, National Team, American Association of Snowboard Instructors

Editor: Isabel Thomas
Cover Design: Michelle Lisseter
Production: Jonathan Smith

Originated by Dot Gradations Ltd
Printed and bound in China and Hong Kong by South China

ISBN 1 844 21290 4
07 06 05 04 03
10 9 8 7 6 5 4 3 2 1

British Library Cataloguing in Publication Data
A catalogue for this book is available from the British Library

Acknowledgements
The publishers would like to thank the following for permission to reproduce photographs:
Rec Sno: p. **1**; SD Tourism/Chad Coppess: pp. **10, 18, 32, 34, 36, 40, 42 top, 43 top**; Unicorn/Mark E. Gibson: pp. **17, 28, 43 bottom**; Unicorn/Dick Young, p. **30**; Corbis: pp. **4, 6, 8, 12–13, 14, 20, 24, 26, 42 bottom**.

Cover photograph reproduced with permission of Corbis.

Every effort has been made to contact copyright holders of any material reproduced in this book. Any omissions will be rectified in subsequent printings if notice is given to the publishers.

Contents

Introduction 4

Snowboarding 8

Getting started 19

Who can become a snowboarder? 27

Who are the professional snowboarders? . . . 31

Competing in snowboarding 37

Quick facts about snowboarding 42

Glossary 44

Internet sites and addresses 46

Books and magazines 47

Index 48

Introduction

Snowboarding is an extreme sport that is growing more and more popular. Many snowboarders ride their special boards down ski slopes. Others ride off jumps and obstacles to do tricks.

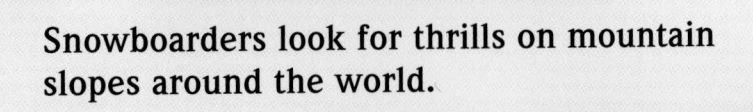

Snowboarders look for thrills on mountain slopes around the world.

Extreme sports are relatively new sports taken up by daring athletes. They are fun, but can also be dangerous. People who take part in extreme sports must do everything they can to be safe and avoid getting injured.

You may have heard of the **X Games**, held every year in the USA. But do you know what a **half-pipe** is? Do you know what a snurfer is or how snowboarding began? Who are the top snowboarders in the world today? What do you need to do if you want to take up the sport? This book will answer all of these questions and more.

How to use this book

This book is divided into parts called chapters. The title of each chapter tells you what it is about. A list of chapters and their page numbers appears on the table of contents on page 3. The index on page 48 gives you the page numbers where you can find the main topics discussed in this book.

Many snowboarders grab their boards
when doing tricks in the air.

Each chapter has colourful photographs, captions and information boxes. The photographs show you some of the things written about in the book, so you can see what they look like. A caption is an explanation that tells you about a photograph. The captions in this book are in pale blue boxes. Special boxes give you extra information about the subject.

You may not know what some of the words in this book mean. To learn new words, you should look them up in a dictionary. This book has a small dictionary called a glossary. Words that appear in **bold** type are explained in the glossary on page 44.

You can use the Internet sites listed on page 46 to learn more about topics discussed in this book. You could write letters to the organizations listed on page 46, asking them questions or asking them to send you helpful information.

Snowboarding

Snowboarding is a cross between surfing and skiing. Snowboarders strap a single wide board to their feet and ride down snow-covered hills or mountains. A snowboard looks like a wide ski.

One of the ways people have fun while snowboarding is by reaching high speeds.

The two main types of snowboarding are **freeriding** and **freestyle**. Freeriders ride their boards down hills and mountain **pistes**. Freestylers use **ramps** to do tricks and jumps on their boards.

A third kind of snowboarding is known as Alpine. These boarders ride on smooth, steep courses and race through slalom gates like ski racers. They also use plastic **boots** like skiers do.

Snowboarders can ride their boards on almost any type of snow. The type of snow they like best is **powder**. Powder is fresh snow that nobody has ridden on yet. It gives a smooth, soft ride and sprays into the air as snowboarders ride it.

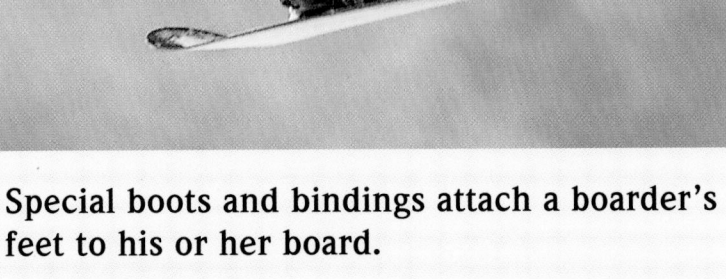

Special boots and bindings attach a boarder's feet to his or her board.

Where do snowboarders ride?

Snowboarders often ride their boards on the same slopes, or pistes, as skiers. When snowboarders and skiers share pistes, they need to follow basic safety rules to avoid each other. In the past, snowboarding was not allowed at many ski resorts. A resort is a place where people go for rest and fun. Since the late 1980s, however, snowboarding has become so popular that many ski resorts have opened their pistes to snowboarders.

A common rule is that a boarder must have a **safety leash** for their board. This ties the snowboard to their body. It stops the board from getting away when the boarder falls over. The safety leash is mainly for step-in **bindings**, which can be released when a boarder is on a ski lift. Bindings are used by snowboarders to fasten their boots to their boards. A loose board sliding down a mountain could injure another boarder or skier. Boarders hold the leashes while walking with their boards.

Snowboarding parks

Many ski resorts have built special parks for snowboarders. These have snow ramps, bumps and jumps that snowboarders can use to do tricks.

Different types of snowboarding

Freeriding is the most popular type of snowboarding. Almost anyone can freeride their board down hills or mountain pistes.

Freeriders can ride their boards however they want, as long as they are safe. Some ride their boards straight down a mountain or hill as fast as they can. Others use bumps on a hill to do tricks on their way down. Freestyling is more difficult. Boarders use ramps to do tricks called **aerials**. Aerials are spins and flips done while the boarder is in the air. Boarders try to jump as high as they can when doing aerials. They call this 'catching air'.

Snowboarders like to ride in fresh snow called powder.

This snowboarder has a safety leash attached to his foot and his board.

How snowboarding began

In the mid 1960s, a man called Sherman Poppen attached two skis together with screws. He tied a rope to the front and rode down a hill. He called his invention the snurfer, a cross between the words 'snow' and 'surfer'. Snurfing became popular in the 1960s and Poppen sold millions of snurfers.

In the 1970s, many surfers and skateboarders tried to improve snurfers. In 1977, Jake Burton started making snowboards. They were made out of wood with a plastic bottom. The plastic helped the boards go quickly through fresh powder snow. He put rubber straps on the top of the boards so riders could tie them to their boots.

Burton's new boards made snowboarding even more popular. He started his own company, which he called Burton. Another snowboarder called Tom Sims also started making snowboards. He called his company Sims. Today, Burton and Sims are two of the most popular makes of snowboard.

Boarder profile: Tom Sims

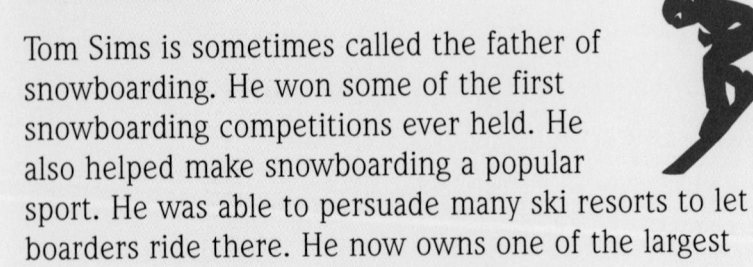

Tom Sims is sometimes called the father of snowboarding. He won some of the first snowboarding competitions ever held. He also helped make snowboarding a popular sport. He was able to persuade many ski resorts to let boarders ride there. He now owns one of the largest snowboard companies in the world – Sims.

Early competitions

In the early 1980s, Burton and Sims helped to start the world's first snowboarding competitions. In 1988, the International Snowboard Federation (ISF) began and started the Snowboarding World Cup. The ISF stopped running in 2002 but the competitions live on.

In 1995, the USA sports television network ESPN started the Extreme Games. Today, this competition is known as the X Games, and it has become the best-known competition for all types of extreme sport. Snowboarders ride in several different freestyle and freeriding events at the X Games. This has helped to make snowboarding a popular sport that is now seen by millions of people on television. In 1998, snowboarding became an Olympic sport.

This snowboarder has caught 'big air' on a slope at a ski resort.

Beginners need to practise often if they want to ride as well as experienced boarders.

Getting started

Pads and guards protect snowboarders when they fall. Hands and wrists are the areas most often injured in falls. Boarders should always wear wrist guards. Wrist guards keep a boarder's wrists straight during a fall and make them less likely to get injured.

Some snowboarders also use **helmets.** The British Snowboarding Association (BSA) recommends that all snowboarders younger than fourteen wear a helmet. Because head injuries can be very serious, every beginner should wear a helmet. Some ski resorts have a rule that snowboarders below a certain age must wear helmets.

The right clothing

Snowboarders need to stay dry and warm, so it is important to choose the right clothes. Boarders can get hypothermia if they become too cold. Hypothermia means a person's body temperature has become dangerously low.

This snowboarder is wearing thick clothes to stay warm and protect the skin.

Wearing layers

Boarders can also get frostbite. Frostbite happens when a person's skin is damaged by extreme cold. Snowboarders should wear several layers of loose clothing, which lets them move quickly and easily. The outside layers should be made of waterproof and windproof material, such as nylon with a waterproof coating.

Board design

Freestyle boards are wide, stable and designed to do tricks on. Freestyle boards also bend easily, so they do not break during tricks. The nose and tail of freestyle boards are the same shape. This lets snowboarders ride forwards or backwards.

Freeriding boards do not bend as easily as freestyle boards. The noses are turned up and they are not as wide as freestyle boards, so they move and turn more easily through powder snow. Some boarders use freeriding boards for racing.

Did you know?

Different types of snow let a boarder ride at different speeds. Wet snow, for example, is sticky. This slows down boarders and makes it harder for them to turn.

Snowboarding safely

Snowboarders should not ride down slopes they think are too steep. Many boarders use the 'falling leaf' way of riding down steep hills. They ride their boards diagonally back and forth across the slope until they reach the bottom. This lets them go as fast or as slowly as they like.

When doing tricks or jumps, boarders must always check in advance where they are going to land. They need to know if they will have to slow down or stop straight after landing. They must also make sure they will not land on a flat piece of ground. They could injure their ankles if they do. An injury is some sort of hurt or damage, like a broken bone or a sprain. A sprain means one of the body's joints has been twisted, tearing its muscles or ligaments. Ligaments hold together the bones in a joint.

Boarders should not ride with their boards flat on the ground. They should always keep the board on one of its edges. If they catch an edge on a bump while riding flat, they will lose their balance and fall over.

Racing boards

Racers ride boards with a flat tail because they only go forwards. Racing boards are the stiffest type of snowboard.

Boots and bindings

Boots strap into the board's bindings. This keeps a snowboarder's feet on the board. Most snowboarders begin with soft boots that bend easily.

Experienced racers use hard boots. The hard outer shell of these boots supports racers' ankles and lets them turn quickly. Hard boots slip into bindings and are held with special clips, like ski boots.

Downhill courses

Most freeride boarders ride downhill on ski pistes. They often use bumps or logs to do tricks. They may drag their boards across them to do spins and turns.

Did you know?

Corn snow is powder that has thawed and then refrozen. It called corn snow because it looks like little sweetcorn kernels. Corn snow is easy for boarders to ride on and helps them to go faster.

Choosing a snowboard

Choosing the right board is important for riding safely and well. Many snowboard makers will make boards exactly how snowboarders want them. Boarders tell the company how they will be riding and the style or colours they would like. The length of the board depends on the height of the rider.

New snowboards can be expensive. Boarders can buy used snowboards for less money. Most resorts will also rent boards. Renting is a good idea for young riders and beginners, especially if they are going to grow between seasons.

Boarders who ride off piste must check out the route they will be riding to make sure it is safe.

Riding off piste

Some freeride boarders leave the main ski pistes and ride through trees on mountain slopes. Most snowboarders who do this are very experienced.

Using ramps

Freestyle snowboarders use different types of ramp to do tricks. **Quarter-pipe** ramps have one curved wall. Half-pipes have two curved walls, shaped like a U. Freestylers try to catch as much air as they can at the top of ramps.

Some boarders want to catch more air than a quarter-pipe or half-pipe will allow. They use **big air** ramps to do tricks. These are shaped like ski jumps. Boarders ride down them to build up speed and jump high into the air to do their tricks.

Boarder profile: Todd Richards

Todd Richards has been a snowboarder since 1990. He was born in the USA in 1969 and lives between Colorado and California. Richards rides mainly in half-pipe competitions. He won two gold medals at the X Games between 1997 and 2000.

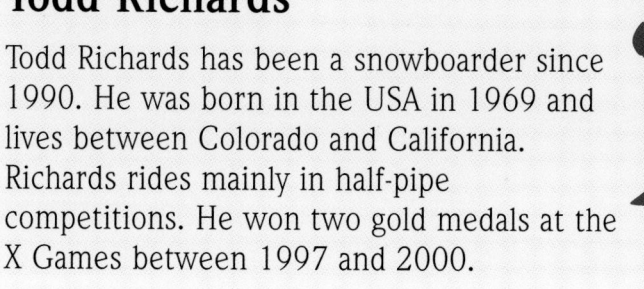

This boarder is using the edge of the board to make a turn across a slope.

Who can become a snowboarder?

Almost anyone can start snowboarding if they prepare properly. It helps to be healthy because snowboarding is an energetic sport. Before beginning, new boarders must find the right snowboard. They also need to learn the safety rules before they learn how to ride well.

Snowboarders use many muscles in their bodies, so warming up is important. Boarders who stretch arm, leg and back muscles get injured less often. They feel more relaxed and awake while riding.

Learning to snowboard

Snowboards have two edges. Stand on your board so that one edge of the snowboard is under your toes and the other edge is under your heels. One of your feet is the front foot while the other is the back foot.

This snowboarder is riding goofy-footed.

Regular and goofy-footed

Most boarders lead with their left foot while riding.
But some lead with their right foot. This is called
riding 'goofy-footed'. You should find out which way is
most comfortable for you and stick with it.

You can start moving by pointing the nose of your board down a slope and leaning forwards. Bend your knees for balance and lean towards the edge of the board that your toes face. Leaning back towards the other side of the board will turn you in the other direction. Riding diagonally back and forth across a hill like this will help you control your speed.

Snowboarders stop quite like ice hockey players do. Bring both feet around so that your board is pointing across the slope of the hill instead of down the hill. Then scrape the board across the snow and move across the hill until you stop.

Where can I train?

Many ski resorts have snowboarding instructors who give lessons to new boarders. You should make sure your instructor belongs to an approved school. The British Snowboard Association (BSA) will help you find a good instructor. Their address is given on page 46 of this book. Most ski areas provide instructors that have been trained to teach people how to snowboard safely.

New snowboarders can also learn and practise on a dry slope or at an indoor snow centre before they try the real thing.

This snowboarder is riding a half-pipe ramp in a competition.

Who are the professional snowboarders?

A **professional**, or pro, is a person who gets paid to do a sport that many people do just for fun. Mathieu Bozzetto is one of the best professional snowboarders in the world. He was born in 1973 in Chambery, France and now lives in Val D'Isere, France. He finished overall second in the 2002 World Cup. This was a result of finishing first in the parallel **slalom**, fifth in the **giant slalom** and second in the parallel giant slalom. Jasey Jay Andersen from Canada finished first overall.

Lesley McKenna is a popular British snowboarder. She was born in Scotland and took up skiing when she was five years old. She became a member of the Scottish Ski Team and later the British Ski Team. She changed to snowboarding when she was twenty years old and was rated number four in the 2002 World Cup standings in half-pipe.

Beginners need to practise before trying tricks like this one.

Practise

Like anyone who wants to learn how to snowboard, Bozzetto and McKenna had to start at the beginning. They practised easy tricks first and then learned more difficult ones. Today, they invent new tricks of their own. Like learning to ride a snowboard, each new trick takes a lot of practise and hard work.

Riding the pipe

To ride **half-pipes**, boarders begin by riding across the pipe to build speed. Then they ride up the wall of the pipe and jump into the air at the top. They try to jump as high as they can to catch air. Boarders who catch more air can do more difficult tricks. Boarders often grab on to their boards when doing tricks.

Big air snowboarders begin by riding down a ski jump or ramp to build up speed. At the bottom of the ramp they jump into the air and do tricks. The bottom of many ramps is often more than 30 metres above the ground. Boarders must land in the right way or they could get hurt.

Snowboarding timeline

1960s: Sherman Poppen invents the snurfer

1977: Jake Burton invents a snowboard

1980s: Jake Burton and Tom Sims start the first snowboarding competitions

1988: First Snowboarding World Cup is held in the USA and Europe

1998: Snowboarding becomes an official sport at the Winter Olympics

This snowboarder is riding regular-footed.

Boarder profile: Jason Borgstede

Jason Borgstede is a well-known big air snowboarder. He won an X Games gold medal in 1998 and a silver medal in 2000. Borgstede was born in St Louis, USA, in 1975. He now lives in Arkansas, USA, when he is not taking part in competitions.

Riding the hill

Some snowboarders like to race. The two types of snowboarding race course are slalom and giant slalom. In slalom competitions, racers ride down different courses next to each other. They use their boards to turn in and out of flags placed along the course. The first snowboarder to reach the bottom of the course is the winner.

In giant slalom competitions, boarders race down a larger course as quickly as they can. The turns are bigger and faster than in slalom races. The winner is the boarder who rides the course fastest.

Most snowboarders are not skilled enough to earn a living from their sport.

Competing in snowboarding

There are lots of competitions for amateur and **professional** snowboarders. British professional competitions take place in Europe and Scotland. There are also indoor and dry slope competitions.

Competitions and prizes

In 1998, some types of snowboarding became Winter Olympic sports. The Winter Olympics take place every four years and are held in a different country each time. Boarders from around the world ride in **slalom** and **freestyle** competitions.

Pro boarders also ride in slalom, freestyle and **big air** events in the **X Games**. The X Games include a competition called the boardercross, or snowboard cross. In it, several boarders race down a slope at the same time. They use jumps and bumps to do tricks on the way down. The first to the bottom is the winner.

Judging events

In freestyle competitions, pro boarders have a set amount of time to ride pipes. Judges give points for the number of tricks they do. Harder tricks get more points. Judges also give boarders points for style and for how high they jump.

Big air snowboarders also receive points for the number of tricks they do. They earn more points for harder tricks and good landings.

Slalom boarders race against a clock. The boarder who takes the least amount of time to finish the course wins the race.

Did you know?

Granular snow is another type of snow that is very difficult to ride on. Like corn snow, granular snow is powder that has thawed and then refrozen, except granular snow refreezes as a flat sheet. This makes it very slippery, almost like riding on ice.

Rankings

Professional boarders earn their living from riding. They try to win prize money at competitions and might earn money from a **sponsor** for wearing certain clothes and equipment. Most ride in national and international competitions all year round. Boarders are ranked by how well they do. The highest ranked boarders ride in the X Games, Winter Olympics and World Championships. Rankings from around the world can be found at www.snowboardranking.com on the Internet.

Boarder profile: Gian Simmen

In 1998, Gian Simmen became the first male snowboarder to win a gold medal in the half-pipe in the Olympics. Simmen is known for his ability to catch big air and do amazing tricks. He was born in 1977 in Switzerland, where he still lives.

Many snowboarders like to be alone on the slopes where they can admire the winter scenery.

Sponsors

A **sponsor** is a business or a person who pays for a snowboarder to ride. The sponsor pays for the boards, clothes and safety equipment. Some sponsors pay for boarders to travel to races around the world.

Many sponsors are makers of snowboards and snowboarding equipment. Boarders wear their sponsor's name on their clothes and boards. Sponsors hope other people will see their name and buy their products. It is a good form of advertising.

A growing sport

Snowboarding has become a very popular extreme sport. Surfers and skateboarders helped bring attention to snowboarding. Many have taken up this sport in addition to their other sports. Each year, snowboarders continue to invent new and better tricks. More and more people watch snowboarding events – in person and on television – every year.

Quick facts about
Snowboarding

- Snowboarders call riding back and forth down a hill 'turning'.

- 'Carving' is when a snowboarder lets the edge of their board slice through the snow while turning.

- 'Skidding' is when a snowboarder lets their board slip sideways across the snow while turning.

- Before ski-style bindings were developed for snowboards, boarders held on to their boards with a rope.

- A snowboarder's bindings are round and shaped to fit the boot. Ski bindings are much longer.

- In 1985, less than half of all downhill ski areas allowed snowboarding on their hills.

- Nicola Thost of Germany won the first snowboarding Olympic gold medal in the women's half-pipe.

Glossary

aerial trick done while catching air

big air type of snowboarding where snowboarders ride down a long narrow ramp to do tricks high in the air

bindings what snowboarders use to fasten their boots to their boards

boot what snowboarders wear over each foot

freeriding style of snowboarding where people ride down a ski run or slope

freestyle style of snowboarding where people ride their boards on jumps to do tricks

giant slalom race down a single obstacle course, done one racer at a time

half-pipe U-shaped ramp with two curved walls

helmet hard type of hat that protects a person's head

piste area on a mountain that has been specially prepared for skiers and snowboarders

powder freshly fallen snow that no one has snowboarded or skied on yet

professional person who makes money doing something
   amateurs do for fun

quarter-pipe ramp with one curved wall used to get
   into the air for tricks

ramp curved surface used for freestyle tricks

safety leash rope or cord attached to a snowboarder's
   board to prevent it from slipping away

slalom snowboarding or ski race down an
   obstacle course

sponsor company who pays someone to use or
   advertise its product

X Games popular extreme sports competition hosted by
   the USA sports television network ESPN

Internet sites and addresses

British Snowboard Association
Hillend
Biggar Road
Mid Lothian, EH10 7EF
Scotland
www.thebsa.org

Snowsport Scotland
www.snsc.demon.co.uk

Soulsports.co.uk
www.soulsports.co.uk

Snowboard Britain.com
www.snowboardbritain.com

British Association of Snowsport Instructors
www.basi.org.uk

International Ski Federation
www.fis-ski.com/snowboarding

Snowlife.org.uk
www.snowlife.org.uk

Books and magazines

Radical sports: Snow Boarding, Sanson, Ian. Heinemann
Library, Oxford, 1999

Snowboarder Magazine
Snowboarding news, features and advice from Europe
and the rest of the world.

Powder Magazine
Skiing magazine with information about resorts,
conditions and technique.

Index

aerial 13

big air 25, 33, 35, 38, 39
binding 11, 23, 42
boot 9, 15, 23, 42

freeriding 9, 13, 16, 21,
    23, 25
freestyle 9, 16, 21, 25,
    38, 39
frostbite 21

giant slalom 31, 35

half-pipe 5, 25, 31, 33,
    39, 43
helmet 19
hypothermia 19

obstacle 4
Olympics 16, 33, 37–39,
    43
powder 9, 15, 21, 38
professional 31, 37

quarter-pipe 25

ramp 9, 13, 22, 25, 33
resort 11, 13, 16, 24, 29

safety leash 11
skiing 8, 9, 11, 31
slalom 31, 35, 38, 39
snurfer 5, 15, 33
sponsor 41
surfing 8

X Games 5, 16, 35, 37, 39